# ENCOUNTERING JESUS AT MASS

## The Treasure of Prayer and the Eucharist

Jeff Smith

**The Word Among Us Press**

9639 Doctor Perry Road

Ijamsville, Maryland  21754

ISBN: 0-932085-25-3

Cover design by Christopher Ranck

Made and printed in the United States of America.

# Contents

# Introduction

How can we come into God's presence and hear his voice? All of us have a hunger that only God can quench as we experience his presence in our hearts. In this book, we want to look at how this hunger can be met through personal prayer and at Mass.

One person who experienced an ever deepening desire for God's presence was Moses. Even after many years of following the Lord, he refused to be content with the degree to which he knew Yahweh. He had already led the Israelites out of Egypt, spent forty days with the Lord on Mount Horeb, and received the ten commandments. Yet, even after all these blessings, Moses still cried out, "If I have found favor in your sight, show me now your ways, that I might know you" (Exodus 33:13). God assured Moses that he would remain with them and give them rest. But Moses was still not satisfied: "If your presence will not go with me, do not carry us up from here" (33:15). The Lord comforted him again, but Moses wanted to know God even more intimately. So, he cried out, "Show me your glory!" (33:18).

Whenever we come to the Lord to pray, either privately or at Mass, we too can plead with the Lord. When God's people cry out and repent of their sin, God hears and answers them. He raised Moses up because the people of Israel cried out for God to rescue them from slavery in Egypt. Later, when the Israelites fled to the mountains to escape their enemies the Midianites, God heard their cries and raised up Gideon to deliver them (Judges 6:6-12).

As we focus on coming into the Lord's presence, let's start on our knees. "O Lord, we beg you to pour your mercy upon us, our families, the church, and the world. We long for you, Jesus. Show us your glory and your love."

Jeff Smith
*The Word Among Us*

# Teach Us to Pray

**A**t *The Word Among Us*, we have been called to encourage people to come into God's presence each day in worship and love. In this book, we want to focus on worshipping God, both in personal prayer and at Mass. In this first chapter, we will consider St. Luke's account of the sinful woman (Luke 7:36-50) and see what we can learn about prayer through this story. As you read these few verses, look for ways in which this woman provides a

touching example of what prayer is all about:
She pursues Jesus; she experiences heart-felt
repentance; she receives forgiveness and mercy;
she bows down in worship; and she offers her
treasure to Jesus.

Everybody in the town knew that she was a
"sinner," and so they shunned her and treated her
like an outcast (Luke 7:37,39). How often she
must have cried out to be saved from the horrible
loneliness that her sin against God and her
neighbors' rejection caused her!

Then came the day when Jesus, a rabbi and
miracle-worker, came to their town. Itinerant
preachers were not uncommon at that time, but
this one drew a huge crowd. He taught with
such authority and love that it was as if the grace
surrounding him permeated the whole crowd.
For the first time in years, this sinful woman was

filled with hope as Jesus' words reached into her heart. "Who is this man? Why is my heart drawn to him? I wonder if anyone else in this crowd feels the way I do?" As the people began to leave, she felt a strong desire to hear more from him and to speak to him herself.

Some time later, she heard that Jesus was visiting Simon, a religious leader of the town. The woman might have been filled with fear, knowing what Simon and his friends thought of her. But hope in Jesus' words drew her to him. She burst into Simon's house and threw herself at Jesus' feet. Tears flooded her eyes—tears of sorrow over her sin and tears of joy in Jesus' presence. "This man knows all about me, but he doesn't draw back."

It seemed as if no one else was in the room. This man loved her in a way no other man ever had. She opened a flask of expensive ointment and poured it out on his feet. "What return can I give to the one who makes me feel so clean? I can give him my most precious treasure. Here, O Lord, is everything I own. I am happy to spend it on you."

## Do I Need Jesus?

The woman's tears were in stark contrast to the reaction of Simon the Pharisee. He had invited Jesus, a fellow rabbi, into his home so that they could discuss their views. Unlike the woman, Simon did not feel any particular need for Jesus. So, when Jesus entered the house, Simon neither embraced him nor extended the customary offer to wash his feet (Luke 7:44-45). He had heard many things about Jesus—both good and bad—

and now he was going to test Jesus' fidelity to the law of Moses.

While the woman wept at Jesus' feet, Simon saw his chance. Under Jewish law, a man became unclean through contact with a prostitute. But that didn't seem to bother Jesus—he let her touch him! Indignant, Simon discarded Jesus' prophetic preaching: "If this man were a prophet, he would have known who and what sort of woman this is" (7:39).

Jesus summed up Simon's response in one simple sentence: "He who is forgiven little, loves little" (Luke 7:47). While this woman's encounter with Jesus resulted in the forgiveness of her many sins, Simon's heart was not changed at all. Because Simon could not see his own need for a savior, he could not understand the love this woman had for Jesus. The woman demonstrated what true faith is all about: pursuing Jesus, heart-felt repentance, receiving forgiveness, worshipping Jesus, and giving one's whole life to the Lord.

## Combining Faith and Prayer

Just as he touched the woman, Jesus wants to deepen our faith. For the sinful woman, approaching Jesus involved her whole being. Even though she had sinned greatly, at that moment when she came face to face with Jesus, she lived out the most important commandment: "Hear, O Israel, You shall love the LORD your God with all of your heart, and with all your soul, and with all your might" (Deuteronomy 6:5). It is this lifting up of our whole being in prayer that is so pleasing to God. Remember the prayer of Mary, the mother of Jesus: "My soul [my whole being] magnifies the Lord and my spirit rejoices in God my Savior" (Luke 1:46-47).

Such a prayer of yielding and vulnerability rises to the throne of heaven as a fragrant aroma of worship. In a story similar to Luke's account of the sinful woman, St. John tells us how Mary, the sister of Martha, took a pound of costly ointment and anointed Jesus' feet, wiping his feet with her hair (John 12:2-8). According to John, "the house was filled with the fragrance of the ointment" (12:3). When we lift our hearts and minds to God, the pleasing fragrance of our prayer rises to the throne of grace. "Through us God spreads the fragrance of the knowledge of him everywhere. For we are the aroma of Christ to God" (2 Corinthians 2:14-15).

Faith is the foundation from which this fragrant aroma rises. It is the foundation of prayer itself.

The sinful woman had learned how to be intimate with her Lord. She could respond because she knew the Lord of love. She experienced the truth behind St. Paul's encouraging words: "For by grace you have been saved through faith; and this is not your own doing—it is the gift of God" (Ephesians 2:8-9).

## Prayer Is a Relationship

Throughout the centuries, many saints have taught their followers various methods of prayer. In your walk of faith, the Lord may have guided you into your own pattern or method of prayer. Be faithful to how the Lord has taught you. Whatever the method, prayer flows first and foremost from an inner relationship with the Holy Spirit. Through the Spirit dwelling in our hearts, Jesus' words become our own: "Thy kingdom come, thy will be done!" No matter how strong or weak they may feel, all Christians have the kingdom of God dwelling richly within them (see Luke 17:21). All Christians can receive the treasures of the kingdom of God and can come to know God intimately through a life of prayer.

At its core, prayer is the communion within the heart that occurs between God and his children. Imagine a married couple in love. Through their outward actions, we can catch a glimpse of their love for each other—they spend time together; they smile at each other; they give up their free time so they can be together. These are but signs of their love. Their true relationship actually occurs deep within their hearts. Similarly, prayer is a relationship that occurs deep within our hearts. It may manifest itself in various actions, such as giving up time to pray and talk with God, or keeping our hearts pure before him. Yet at its core, prayer is a relationship.

Through prayer, our relationship with God can grow and mature. As we continue in prayer, we will begin to sense the presence of the Lord more often. Like a thick cloud, his presence will lead us to deeper worship and love for God. Like the sinful woman who "wasted" her most prized possession on Jesus, we come before Jesus, weep over our sins and those of the world, and lay down all of our treasures before the Lord. Our treasures may include our reputation, our security, or our comfort. Whatever they are, we place them at Jesus' feet and we worship him.

# Teach Us to Pray!

Prayer is a gift from God. It is not something we do for him, but a beautiful gift that he bestows on us as we humbly seek his presence. Having learned from this sinful woman, let us seek Jesus every day with the same love that compelled her.

"O blessed sinful woman, how blessed you were to have kissed our Master's feet! What a privilege to have wept before him in repentance and love! Yet, we too can know this same privilege. We can love Jesus in spirit and truth because the Holy Spirit within us loves to spend time in God's presence. We can wait for Jesus in prayer. We can weep at his feet because of our sin and the sin of the world. Thank you, Jesus, for giving us your Spirit and inviting us into a relationship of love with you and your Father. Lord, teach us to pray."

# Invited to the Banquet

**T**he heavenly Father loves to spend time with his children. As we come together for Sunday Mass, how happy he must be to see his children gather around his table! If we as human beings desire to gather our families together, how much more must our God rejoice when his family comes together. In this chapter, we want to examine our disposition and attitudes as we come to Mass. Are we prepared to receive everything that our Father has in store for us?

Early in their marriage, Bob and Kathy McCarthy felt that it was important to teach their children the importance of being a family. So they set aside Sunday as a special day for the whole family to spend together. After church, they would spend the day playing games and having fun with each other. The day was always capped with a special dinner.

Even after their children had married and started their own families, the whole McCarthy family continued to gather every Sunday. Everyone looked forward to the feast. Grandpa especially loved holding their newest grand-child, Bobby, in his arms, and marveling at their resemblance. As time went by, the married children came to enjoy their time with their parents more and more. They didn't attend because their presence was expected. They came because they loved their parents and all they had done for them.

We can use this analogy to give us a glimpse of what Sunday Mass can become for us. Every Sunday, our heavenly Father invites us to his house where we can spend time in his presence and hear his voice. Receiving the body and blood of Christ is not something that we simply do. In the Eucharist, we come face to face with Jesus, the Lord of the universe. Every time we come to the table, we can spend precious time in God's presence. How vital it is, then, that our hearts are set on the Lord. Otherwise, we might miss the abundant gifts and joy that God delights to give us.

When our hearts and minds are gazing on the risen Christ, Mass can become a time of deep adoration and praise. The liturgy contains all the major components of prayer: repenting of our sin; hearing God's voice in the scriptures; proclaiming who God is in the creed; interceding with the power and authority of children of God; meeting the Lord personally at the Eucharistic feast; and worshipping and offering him thanks. During all these moments, grace and spiritual gifts flow from heaven. Such grace is only limited by the attitude and disposition of our hearts.

## A Time of Worship

We have two choices when we come to Mass: We can 'go through the motions,' reciting the prayers but remaining distant from God. Or, we can have a life-changing encounter with the living God. Jesus wants so much more than our attendance. Like a bridegroom gazing at his beautiful bride, he longs for intimacy with his people. Every gathering at Mass is a precursor to the marriage feast of the Lamb, when Jesus will return to gather the church to himself and present her holy and blameless before his Father. As the bride of Christ, we belong to Jesus, and we come together at Mass to celebrate our bridegroom and receive his love.

The Holy Spirit delights in revealing these wonderful truths to us and planting them within our hearts. During times of worship such as these, when our hearts are open to receiving life from the Spirit, the promise of scripture is fulfilled: "God is love, and he who abides in love abides in God, and God abides in him" (1 John 4:16). This is what our experience of liturgy should be. "O Spirit of Christ, come to all of us in a new and mighty way today. Help us to pray.

Give us a vision of heavenly things. Help us to see Jesus, our bridegroom, crowned with glory and honor!"

## Called Together for Worship

*He chose us in him before the foundation of the world, that we should be holy and blameless before him.* (Ephesians 1:4)

Every one of us has a special calling that God prepared for us before the beginning of creation. He has given each of us special gifts and called us to use them to build his kingdom. But beyond our individual callings, God has called us together as the body of Christ to worship him in love and unity. At Mass, he calls us together and empowers us to be good stewards of our gifts.

When you come into God's presence, do you sense this call? The early apostles knew it.

Jesus called them from all walks of life. He taught them and loved them and formed them, ultimately drawing them to the intimacy of the last supper. His call brought unity to an unlikely lot: A tax collector and Roman collaborator sat down at table with tradesmen who were forced to pay Roman taxes that they despised. Today, the invitation is just as powerful. Jesus Christ, the supreme Lord over the church and all creation, calls to us every week: "I stand at the door and knock" (Revelation 3:20).

Consider the many blessings that have been received in the context of the Mass. The early church experienced the Eucharist as a time when members of the body of Christ prayed together for the whole church, for her people, and for her mission. When the first Christians gathered for the agapé meal, they came together for fellowship, to receive teaching, to pray together, and to celebrate "the breaking of bread" (Acts 2:42).

Jesus encouraged his disciples to pray together and to expect prayers to be powerfully answered for the whole church, for "where two or three are gathered in my name, there am I in the midst of them" (Matthew 18:20). When we consider the millions of baptized faithful praying together on Sundays, it is evident that our prayers offered together extend throughout the whole church. Each believer receives grace and blessing from the prayer and worship of the whole church.

## A Spiritual Battle

Every time we come before God at Mass, we face many obstacles. Distracting thoughts flood our minds. Plans for the day can threaten to push Jesus aside. Different attitudes—from boredom to anxiety to frustration with the demands of life—can keep us from encountering God deeply. Have you ever thought, "I need to 'get Mass in' so that I can get to do something I really want to do"? Tiredness and passivity can prowl around our hearts like thieves seeking to rob us of our experience of the presence of God. This is why we need to examine our disposition and attitudes. Do I approach Sunday Mass with an expectancy and a desire to encounter the Lord who loves me deeply? Am I eager to see God work in my heart and in those around me?

In addition to this battle for our minds, we are also engaged in a spiritual battle during Mass. Satan is constantly trying to disrupt our time of prayer by introducing little doubts into our minds about whether it is even possible to experience God and hear his voice in our hearts. He urges us away from prayer, worship, and unity with the people of God. He knows that if he can convince us to isolate ourselves from God and from our brothers and sisters, we will miss out on the blessings God has reserved for us in the heavenly realm. The evil one hates worship of God, and he will take advantage of our minds' reluctance to enter into the presence of God in prayer.

God's call to us at Mass is irresistible. He calls us to pray, to worship, to enter into the very presence of the Blessed Trinity. Like a loving Father, he delights in teaching us, forming us in his wisdom, and pouring out his love upon us. Every time we gather to celebrate the Eucharist, we can experience the blessings of being members of his family, sons and daughters of God.

In the next chapter, we will examine the various segments of the Mass to understand how

each part—the scripture readings, the interces-
sions, the Eucharistic prayer, and communion—is
intended to draw us closer to God's throne of
grace.

# Take and Eat

**I**n the previous chapter, we examined the disposition and attitude we should have as we approach the Eucharistic feast. In this chapter, we want to mine some of the treasures that are available in the liturgy for those who come to the altar with open, thirsty hearts. In each section of the Mass—from the Penitential Rite and the Liturgy of the

Word through the Eucharistic Prayer and Communion—Jesus eagerly awaits us, ready to reveal heavenly mysteries.

## "I Confess . . ."

God's promises are as strong and dependable as granite. His love for us never diminishes. So in the liturgy, we enter the door to God's presence as we repent of our sins. With the humility of a servant, Jesus cleanses us. He breaks the power of sin and removes the chains of guilt, enabling us to enter God's presence.

Try to visualize Jesus as he washed the feet of his disciples (see John 13:1-11). He told them that they did not need to have their bodies washed, only their feet . Similarly, we do not need the complete bath that we received in baptism—but we do need to be washed clean of the sins of self-love that dirty our feet each day. Whether through judgmental thoughts of the mind or angry outbursts of our tongues, we all sin. And yet, these transgressions do not wipe out the miracle of forgiveness that we received in baptism.

Satan will do anything to keep us from repentance. In his attempts to minimize sin, he will whisper to us, "Don't worry about that little thing; you have a right to be angry toward that person." But, however big or small it is, our sin saddens God because it hinders the intimacy that he wants to have with us.

As you come to Mass, be courageous. Face your sin and repent of it. Come to your Father and ask his forgiveness. Repent of any dispositions that prevent you from having a close friendship with him. Tell him that you are sorry for any angers, fears, lustful thoughts or actions, or even apathy toward God. From the very start of Mass, you will find freedom to enter the throne room of God.

## The Living Word

The writer of the letter to the Hebrews tells us, "The word of God is living and active, sharper than any two-edged sword . . . discerning the thoughts and intentions of the heart" (Hebrews 4:12). God wants to cut away from our hearts all that is false (sin) and replace it with the truth. When we are eager and attentive, the Spirit of God can speak to us in the scripture readings and reveal God's mind to us. When they met the risen Jesus on the road to Emmaus, two of his disciples were pierced to the heart as he explained the scriptures to them (Luke 24:32). The same can be true for us. When we hear God's word, our hearts can burn with love as the truth penetrates our minds.

"Hearing" God's word can be quite different from "listening" to it. Hearing is limited to our ears receiving sound waves and sending signals to the brain for interpretation. But listening requires that we pay close attention. We may sometimes think, "I listen, but how can I hear God speaking to me?" This is why we have to trust that when we quiet our hearts and listen to his word, God, who loves us dearly, will surely speak words of comfort, correction, and peace to us.

Lack of contact with scripture can cause our hearts to grow cold toward God. Conversely, when we allow his word to penetrate our hearts, we will hear the Spirit speaking gently to us. When we are convinced that the scriptures are "truth" rather than just another opinion, confusion will give way to clarity, and our actions will flow from God's word rather than from our feelings.

## "I Am the Bread of Life"

The Liturgy of the Eucharist is a time when we can come face-to-face, heart-to-heart, with Jesus. By exercising our faith, we can truly encounter Jesus in the consecrated bread and wine. When we are content with our own reason, we risk missing the wonder and intimacy of this encounter.

The early church faced the same challenge we face today. Both Sts. Paul and John warned their followers to have the right heart in their celebrations of the Eucharist. When the Corinthians took the communion table lightly, Paul wrote sternly, "Whoever, therefore, eats the bread or drinks the cup of the Lord in an unworthy manner will be guilty of profaning the body and blood of the Lord" (1 Corinthians 11:27). It is truly wonderful that millions receive the body of Christ each week. And yet, Paul's words still confront us all: Do we come to the table worthily, with a deep desire to receive life from Jesus?

In his teaching on the Eucharist, St. John wrote of a growing tension between Jesus and many of his followers (John 6:1-71). When he miraculously fed five thousand people with only a few loaves of bread, Jesus gave his disciples a sign of the bread of life that he would become for all of them. And yet, on the next day, most of these disciples could not accept his teaching.

They tried to make Jesus' words fit into the categories of human reason, but Jesus was trying to raise them up to the heavenly realm: "Do not labor for the food which perishes, but for the food which endures to eternal life, which the Son of man will give to you" (6:27).

The people's response showed that they placed their confidence in themselves more than in the grace of God: "What must we do, to be doing the works of God?" (6:28). But Jesus continued to urge them (and us) to rely on the truth and trust in God: "Just believe in me. Stay close to me, rely on me, abide in me" (see 6:29). Jesus is always seeking to raise his followers up to the heavenly realm; he always teaches on a spiritual plane. Every time we approach the altar, we should recall Jesus' promise: "I am the bread of life; he who comes to me shall not hunger, and he who believes in me shall never thirst" (John 6:35).

## Communion and the Cross of Christ

As he gathered with his disciples in the upper room, Jesus knew that his time was drawing near. The Passover meal that he shared with them that night was a feast of love between him and his closest friends. Today, the Eucharist remains a feast of love between Jesus and all of us, whom he longs to call his friends (John 15:15).

At the last supper, Jesus told his disciples, "Do this in remembrance of me" (Luke 22:19). May we never forget that Jesus is our bread. He is our life, our hope, and our truth. As we partake of the bread of life, Jesus wants to raise our minds to the heavenly realm. He wants us to imagine ourselves at the heavenly banquet, seated at table with Jesus and all his people. When we come face to face with the Lord in the presence of all the angels and saints, how can we help but worship him and thank him for everything that he has done for us?

After you have received Jesus' body and blood, spend a few minutes gazing at the cross in the sanctuary. We can receive Jesus in this marvelous way only because he shed his blood for us at Calvary. What pain must have consumed the Father's heart as he watched his only Son die like a thief! And yet, how his heart must have been filled with love for humanity and all creation. It is finally accomplished! The mystery of God's love has conquered sin. In the cross, we see both incredible beauty and unimaginable suffering. When we gaze on the cross with eyes of faith, we can see the love and healing that Jesus offers us every time we receive his body and blood.

What more can we say about the treasures of the liturgy? Jesus offers so much more than we could ever express. How powerful it is when God's children cry out, "Our Father"! How pleasing it is when they offer each other the kiss of peace. We could spend hours dwelling on the truths proclaimed in the creed. Every time you come to Mass, may you be satisfied with nothing less than meeting Jesus, worshipping him, and receiving his grace.

# *Remembering Calvary*

We receive many of the greatest treasures of the liturgy as we recall the central events of Jesus' life. One of the greatest is his cross and resurrection. Scripture tells us that Jesus died in our place. *We* were the guilty ones, but *he* took upon himself our guilt and shame. His death on the cross was for *us*. Then, having completed his mission, Jesus rose from the dead, victorious over all sin and darkness. Because of the cross, we are reconciled to God!

# *Keys to Better Prayer*

**Pursue Jesus. (Luke 7:37)**
Just as the sinful woman burst in to see Jesus, we can eagerly seek him out every day in prayer. Pursue him. Spend time with him. Don't let fear or guilt keep you from entering into his presence.

**Repent from the heart. (Luke 7:38)**
The woman's tears spoke more to Jesus than her words. Weep for your sins and the sins of the world as you kneel at the feet of the Savior.

**Receive Jesus' forgiveness. (Luke 7:50)**
Jesus will never draw away from you or reject you. He delights in forgiving all your sins, however little or big they may be.

**Worship Jesus. (Luke 7:45)**
Stay at Jesus' feet for a few minutes longer than usual. Worship and adore the Lord over all creation. His love for you endures forever.

**Offer your whole life to Jesus. (Luke 7:46)**
Tell the Lord that he is your greatest treasure. Freely offer him all the other treasures in your life. Lay everything at his feet.

# Examining Your Heart
# Before Mass

If possible, try to get to church ten or fifteen
minutes before Mass starts to prepare your heart for
all that God intends to pour upon you during the
liturgy. Take some time to ponder the following
questions and to settle your heart in God's presence.

1.) Do I have a sense of expectancy that God is
inviting me to a banquet when I come to Mass?

2.) What are my motivations for coming to Mass?
Do I come out of a sense of duty? Or can I see
Mass as an opportunity to spend time with
the Lord?

3.) What thoughts or attitudes keep me from lifting up my heart to God during Mass? Do I recognize the spiritual battle in which the evil one wants to rob me of my sense of God's presence?

4.) Am I ready—to the best of my ability—to worship the Lord with my whole heart during Mass?

5.) Do I have a sense that the whole family of God is coming to worship and rejoice in God's presence?